Free and Clear How to Master Your Money and Escape the Debt Trap

Deborah Gorman

Copyright © 2015 Deborah Gorman
 Revised Second Edition
First Published by Deborah Gorman at Smashwords.com
Free and Clear: Break the Debt Habit and Gain Financial Liberation,
Cover art by Thomas Gorman
Copyright 2009

All rights reserved.
ISBN: 1511813598
ISBN-13: 978-1511813594

DEDICATION

In memory of my parents, Thomas F. Gorman and Alice Schutt Gorman.

CONTENTS

	Introduction	i
1	Finding Your Bottom Line	1
2	The Spending Trail	Pg 12
3	Choices and Decisions	Pg 15
4	Evaluate Your Situation and Chart Your Course	Pg 21
5	Pay Yourself First	Pg 26
6	One Step at a Time	Pg 31
7	Crunch Time	Pg 34
8	Complications and Trade Offs	Pg 38
9	Get Help if You Need It	Pg 41
10	Is Bankruptcy An Option?	Pg 44
11	The Courage to Change	Pg 47
12	The Unbroken Circle	Pg 49
13	Gratitude-- Thanksgiving	Pg 51
	Resources	Pg 53
	About Deborah Gorman	Pg 57

INTRODUCTION

"We aren't poor, we're just broke."
Like a hamster endlessly running on a spinning wheel, you're going nowhere. Some months things seem to go along ok, but then an emergency comes along. You take a flat tire in to be fixed, and the mechanic informs you he's not allowed to fix tires with so little tread left. But the other three tires aren't much better. So you decide to buy a replacement set of four tires. Of course it is a necessity. Charging them to a credit card will add a couple hundred dollars to your balance on EZ Money Card, but as long as you can keep making your minimum monthly payments, it will work out.

Yet as each new emergency piles another burden on top of your load, you find yourself living with a vague sense of uneasiness that things will never work out. At times you are so burdened with worry over money it's hard to sleep. You never thought life could be so stressful, at least financially.

If you're constantly living from paycheck to paycheck, what would happen if your income were unexpectedly cut off for any reason? How would you manage to make the payments and your other living expenses?

How did you get here? What can you do to regain a solid financial footing?

Amazingly some of us have never stopped to consider those questions. As a pastor I knew the financial problems some parishioners faced. That experience also made me aware that money is an issue that is deeply private for most people. Indebtedness and financial insolvency carry much baggage and burden individuals with embarrassment, guilt and shame.

I have counseled young couples preparing for marriage who had virtually all of their income committed to payments of various kinds, yet they had never considered what might happen if they suddenly suffered a reversal of fortune in the event of a job loss or other mishap. They simply assumed that would not happen.

The financial melt down and economic recession that started in 2007 with the collapse of the real estate bubble brought that reality crashing down on millions of people.

I have also experienced my own financial crisis times. I write from having known the deep pain and fear that comes with financial distress caused by being overextended, and worked my way out of it.

I have been on the brink of foreclosure and flirted with bankruptcy from being overextended with credit card debt. When I finished graduate school I was heavily in debt, was turned down for credit cards, and unable to get a car loan. But I learned how to manage my money, and I was able to overcome my money troubles.

After I worked through repayment of all of my student loans, I then achieved financial solvency with no debts and money saved for a rainy day and retirement.

In this book I hope to share what I have learned from my own experience with financial struggles.

1 Finding Your Bottom Line

"The best way out is always through." — Robert Frost
What is your present financial situation? Where are you headed? How will you get there? Do you have any financial plan?

If you know you have money problems, but otherwise have no answers for those questions, then it may be time to examine your finances in detail to get an accurate picture of where you are. Facing your finances will help you to decide what steps you need take to achieve financial freedom.

Creating a Financial Balance Sheet will show you how much money you have versus how much you owe.

The first step is to draw up an itemized list of all of your financial assets.

Include cash on hand, money in checking or savings accounts, as well as any funds in IRA or 401K accounts, and or stocks that you own. Add up all of these to determine your Total Assets.

Second, gather all of your bills together, including utilities, insurance, mortgage payment or rent, car loans, credit cards, and any other debts such as back taxes, student loans, credit card balances or medical bills. These are your Total Liabilities.

Then, add together the totals of all of your assets, including your retirement accounts with the others, and any equity in a house or car, then subtract your total liabilities, and you will arrive at your Total Net Worth.

At this point your overall financial picture should be more clearly in focus. Setting aside for the time being your basic monthly income and expense needs, your Total Net Worth is the amount you would have left if you were to use all of your assets to pay off your liabilities.

If your Total Net Worth is a positive number, that's good. Your financial health may be better than you had thought. But if you found that your net worth is a negative number, or if you constantly come up short with your monthly expenses, then you have two options. You can just continue to drift along and hope that things get better. Or you can decide to take action to improve the situation and get back on track.

So here you are. This may not be where you want to be, but it is what it is. Not surprisingly, your assessment has confirmed the deficit in your personal finances. You are caught in the cash flow crunch, with too much month left at the end of the money. The pressure is building. You feel like you are being squeezed in a gigantic vise. You've painted yourself into a corner, and you can see no way out. Take heart.

While your prospects at present appear bleak, you have taken an important first step toward escaping from the financial trap you are in. You have had the courage to face the painful details of your finances and get an accurate picture of where you stand.

What to do?
 * Win the lottery?
 * Rob a bank?
 * Declare bankruptcy?
 * Refinance by taking out a new loan?
 * Walk away from it, disappear and get a new identity?

None of these is a good choice. They are either unrealistic or will lead to additional troubles.

At this point finding the solution to your financial crisis is something that only you can accomplish. You need to tap in to an unused, though potentially powerful resource that is available to you. There is only one person who can solve this problem and get you out of this mess, and that is you.

The most valuable, powerful ability you have to obtain financial freedom is your own decision.

The choice is yours. Either you decide that you will overcome your financial problems and gain financial freedom, or you will stay trapped, in the quicksand of debt. You have already taken the first tentative baby steps toward escaping from the pit you're in and resolving your problems. If you desire to dig your way out of the financial hole, then your first step is to decide that you intend to change the way you conduct your finances. You must take charge. You must make a deliberate decision to take responsibility for your finances. Making a firm, definite decision will be crucial to your turnaround.

Once you have decided to take charge, you must follow through, and focus on making an action plan. Resolve to take action and make the changes required to reverse your fortunes.

Of course if you are married, the decision must be made jointly with your spouse and children if you have any. Because even if one partner takes care of financial matters, it is essential to involve everyone in the family in discussing the problem as well as planning and carrying out solutions. You will need to reach a mutual understanding of your financial situation, and come to an agreement on how to resolve it that will preserve unity and harmony within your family. Only if every family member is involved can you expect to succeed.

2 The Spending Trail—Where Has All Your Money Gone?

"Beginning is half done."-- Cicero

Once you have decided to reverse the course of your finances, the next step is to find out where your money is actually going. Many of us have been careless about financial record-keeping, and so we do not know what our monthly expenditures are.

If you're like me, perhaps even the idea of budgeting sounds boring. That was my mindset. I had always disliked bookkeeping and accounting. My eyes would start to glaze over at the thought of an accounting ledger or spread sheet. So I would procrastinate and postpone bookkeeping tasks, and just muddle along. Such laziness costs dearly in the long run though. As a result I usually had only a vague idea of the state of my finances. But in order to change my situation, I had to face my finances.

After you have calculated at your net worth, you will need to get an accurate picture of your monthly cash flow needs.

Step One: Calculate your total monthly income after tax and any other deductions. Include all household income from any source, including salary, part-time employment, and any miscellaneous income that you receive.

Step Two: Separate your recurring monthly short-term expenses from other long-term debts that you owe such as home mortgage or car loans, and the total balances due on credit card and other debts that are paid over time.

To get an accurate picture of your current expenses, you will need to make a record of all of your spending for each month. That includes not only the larger payments for housing, insurance, utility bills and so on, but also the smallest amount you spend each day.

Every member of the family should be involved in this project. Save all of your receipts. Keep a small notebook where you jot down any miscellaneous amounts where you don't get a receipt. If you buy a coffee and roll at the convenience store in the morning, write that down; fast food at the drive-through for lunch, enter that too; gas or other commuting expense, laundry or dry-cleaning.

Gather all of your receipts and notes together and tally these up at the end of the week, and then add each week's totals to find your spending for the month. You may be surprised when you see how much money goes for little things.

Once you have a complete record of what you are spending, you will be able to easily track your expenditures.

Sample Expense Ledger

   Date   Category   Amount

   _____
   _____
   _____
   _____
   _____
   _____

Be sure to enter the amount for each expense, including cash. We'll come back to this record again once it is filled in to analyze it in more detail. That's all there is to it.

Step Three: Add up all the payments you are expected to make each month, including all of your living expenses, such as groceries, gas and commuting, prescriptions, household expense, utilities, insurance, clothing, and entertainment.

Then compare the two totals of monthly expenses and income to create a rough working idea of your monthly budget or spending plan, if you prefer that term.

To get a precise idea of your average monthly expenses, you should do this for at least three months, before you set up your Spending Plan. Just starting to keep track of your expenses will give you more awareness about where your money is going. The knowledge that you gain will help you to take charge and make better decisions about your money. Keeping track of your expenses should become regular habit.

3 Choices and Decisions

"If you don't know where you are going, any road will take you there." — Lewis Carroll

Brian and Elaine, a couple I once knew, found themselves in financial distress. Both of them were working and had good jobs, their children were grown and no longer living at home. Yet every month they found themselves struggling to pay their bills. Because of their busy schedules, they had gotten into the habit of eating most of their meals out in restaurants, but they had never considered how much it cost them to do so.

Since they had only a vague idea of how much they were spending, they didn't realize how much they actually spent on their meals.

Not paying attention to how we spend our money is a common cause of money problems. Before you can solve your financial problem, you will first have to find out exactly where your money is going.

After you have arrived at your net worth, the next step is to establish your monthly cash flow needs.

Then, if your bill payments and expenses exceed your income, or your net worth is negative you will need to find a way to balance your expenses and income. Your challenge is how to solve the equation.

A possibility is to earn enough additional income so that you're able to cover all your monthly expenses. That's logical, right? This is simply a cash flow problem and the obvious solution would seem to be to increase your income. Most people who are challenged financially believe that their problem is simply one of not having enough money.

Because the issue may at first seem to be one of insufficient income or cash flow to meet their needs, they say, "If only I had more money coming in, all would be well."

To increase their income, they may look around for a chance to get a second job in the off hours when they aren't working. Perhaps it is time to seek a better paying job, or negotiate a raise at one's present job. So usually this is a starting point.

Certainly getting a raise or a better-paying job or profession is a worthwhile goal. However, increasing your income usually takes some time. Getting into a better job or profession may require additional education or training, which can be costly and take months or years to complete. Meanwhile you are still facing the immediate problem of how to address your financial shortfall. There are, however, steps you can take immediately that will improve your situation.

Although financial problems may initially appear to result from insufficient income, often that shortfall is not the only cause. Many individuals increase their income, only to discover that they are still burdened with the same financial troubles. Their additional earnings have failed to resolve their problems with debt management. They then discover that insufficient income alone is not the problem. Simply having more money doesn't solve their financial distress. While inadequate income or under-earning are real issues that need to be addressed before you can obtain financial solvency, the problem of overspending can be equally to blame.

An estimated one third of lottery winners file for bankruptcy at some point after receiving their windfall. Seventy-eight percent of NFL players file for bankruptcy, get divorced or are unemployed within two years of their last game.

If you have already increased your income either by getting more work, a raise or a better job, and you still find yourself continuing to coming up short, then your money problems are most likely caused by overspending rather than a shortage of money.

Under-earning and overspending are the two root causes of financial hardship, and are usually intertwined as contributing factors to financial crisis.

In either case you will need to take a closer look at your finances to determine the exact cause of your problem, and then devise a plan to solve it. To find a cure for your financial headache, you will need to make some decisions. You have now reached a critical point. If you're reading this book because you are living in daily financial chaos, making the necessary changes will not be easy. If it were, you wouldn't be in the hole. Unfortunately, there is no instant remedy. Solving your financial problems will take determination and time. Only you can decide if you are willing to pay the price to turn your finances around, because you will need to make many changes if you are going to succeed.

Making a definite decision to change is the place to begin to turn your fortunes around. Again I emphasize the decision is yours.

Financial problems are not caused by money, or the lack thereof, but rather by our attitude toward money. Resolving your financial problems will require a fundamental change in your thinking. Out of control spending habits result from our attitudes, thoughts and feelings.

Our attitude about money is the root of any financial problem. The question of attitude is critical, because that is where the problem begins. If you've had a careless attitude about money, and haven't really paid attention to how you have been spending your money and what you have spent it on, that is one reason you are where you are today.

You may even have tried making a budget once or twice, but it didn't work.

We're all creatures of habit, and once we get in a rut, it can be like having blinders on. We just keep charging straight ahead down the same path without looking to either side. Perhaps we have become so dependent on credit that we can't imagine living without it. We have no vision of an alternative way.

So we keep procrastinating, postponing the day of reckoning until we reach some crisis point from which we can get a glimpse of our impending financial ruin.

We may have believed that once we reach our credit limit we will have to stop. But as long as we haven't quite gotten that far, we stay on the same path, maintaining our usual spending patterns.

As you approach your available credit limit, you may start paying a bit more to bring down your balance. Oddly enough, just as you approached that point, the card companies may have even increased your limit, or you were able to obtain temporary relief by opening a new card account with a balance transfer offer of lower interest for so many months.

Zero interest for a year on balance transfers, or very low interest rates can be quite enticing to an over-extended borrower. Such offers may temporarily lull you into a false sense of well being. They may have led you to believe that perhaps your situation is not so bad after all, or the companies would not be further extending your credit. But in the long run, such gimmicks have only postponed the inevitable day of reckoning.

Over-spending and borrowing patterns have settled into our lives as daily necessities almost like an addiction. What is worse, it affects our health, causing anxiety, depression and loss of sleep.

Because of our dependency on credit we may have come to believe that it would be impossible for us to live any other way; we are afraid, stressed out and terrified of the consequences of living without it.

We need to get a grip and realize that it is entirely possible to escape the debt trap and avoid disaster. It may not be easy, and it certainly will take time, but it can be done. There are alternatives to being dependent on credit and incurring debt. The idea that using credit and incurring unsecured debt is a necessity is a myth.

Therefore, in order to overcome the paralysis that results from our fears of looming financial disaster, we must believe that we can turn our situation around. We must believe that it is possible to escape our present bondage and obtain a secure future, free of debt.

First and foremost, we need to make a firm decision that we will no longer rely on unsecured borrowing to meet our financial needs. We will need to create a vision of our destination, an image of financial security, as well as the confidence that we can achieve our goal.

If you have decided that you're tired of living in chaos and desire to find an exit, it helps to frame the alternative, not as a fearful, painful, stifling reality, but rather as a liberating, healthy, positive improvement in your quality of life.

No longer will you be stressed out from the constant nagging and harassment of collection agencies, overdue notices and penalties, or burdened with compound interest charges. Instead you will have peace of mind, security and confidence.

Visualize what your future could be like if you succeed in gaining financial freedom.

Imagine yourself being debt free with money in savings, and enough money to invest in a home if you desire, for your children's education, and your own retirement. More importantly, picture yourself being serene, secure, and confident. Your future will be brighter, once you are on a solid financial foundation.

This moment is both a challenge and an opportunity for you. Don't squander it. Use it for all it's worth.

Once you have arrived at your point of decision, you will want to put a plan down in writing so that you will have it available for future reference.

Keeping in mind your vision for your financial future, write it out as your personal Statement of Purpose that clearly states your objective along with the steps you plan to take to achieve it. Forming definite goals can be a powerful tool to help you stay focused on your vision. Although goals are important, they are not magical, and merely establishing goals does not mean that they will automatically be fulfilled. "Whatever the mind of man can conceive and believe, it can achieve." — Napoleon Hill

As you advance on the course you have set for yourself, there will be numerous obstacles along the way. You will meet setbacks, disappointments and discouragement.

Having a vision and goals in mind as you encounter them will be crucial to your success.

Make your goals definite by establishing dates for achieving them. For example, by one year from now, I intend to pay off A, B, and C balances, and have $X amount in savings. After you have written it out, keep the plan in a handy place and refer to it every day, reading it first thing in the morning, and at night before you retire. If you find that you are not able to achieve your goal within the original timeframe you have established, don't give up. Goals are only benchmarks; and the date you set to reach them can always be revised. If you do not reach them this year, there's always next year.

4 Evaluate Your Situation and Chart Your Course

"Both poverty and riches are the offspring of thought." — Napoleon Hill

Now that you know where your money is going, it's time to evaluate your financial information.

Take a close look at the items on the list of your recorded expenses. Then go down your list of payments, and place a check mark beside each item that was essentialNow take this list of your monthly expenses, and divide them into categories such as living expense, car expense, health, debt payment and so on. Combine related items together in groups such as car-transportation, or food, household, to find a rough estimate of your monthly expense for those categories. . All spending, including non-essential items should be included in the categories, The check marks help you to find areas of overspending to be trimmed.

Next, make a second list that shows all of your regular expenses for the month. This will become the basis of your Spending Plan. This includes three parts: Expenses, Income, and Creditors.

Now compare the Total for all of your Expenses with your Total Monthly Income.

Expenses
Category   Amount
_____
_____
_____
_____

Income
Category   Amount

14

_____
_____
_____
_____

Creditors
Category   Amount

_____
_____
_____
_____

If your regular monthly expenses are less than your monthly income, hurray! Bringing your finances into balance will be much easier. If, on the other hand, your regular expenses are greater than your income, it will be more of a challenge to resolve. In any case, the next step is the same.

You are now ready to take a closer look at your spending list to find out where all the money you spend is going. You can enter individual expenditures into groups such as Dining out, Entertainment, Miscellaneous, Clothing, and so on.

You may be surprised by what this exercise reveals. Many people have no idea how much they have been spending or where their money has been going.

The next step is to decide how much you can afford to spend on any non-essentials. If you are in very dire straits financially, perhaps many or most of them will either have to be cut out altogether or else drastically reduced.

It may be impossible to eliminate them entirely, but look for ways to cut back. For example, if you have been eating out frequently, perhaps you might change to going out once a month, and then set a budget amount for that.

Food is one area that offers many choices and opportunities for adjusting your spending habits. Depending on how often you eat out in restaurants or fast food places, a sizable amount of savings may be awaiting you here, that you can now begin to use for paying down your bills and debts. Shopping for groceries and preparing your own meals at home is far more economical than eating out. Make a weekly meal plan, and only buy the items that you need each week. It's not necessary to buy more than you need by buying extra items beyond the basics to stock your pantry and refrigerator.

Give yourself an allowance. It is unrealistic expect to eliminate all nonessential spending.

Austerity does not work. Trying to totally cut out all extras can backfire by creating too much frustration, and result in negative feelings and a defeatist attitude, especially if you are prone to binge spending or shopping sprees to give yourself a mood lift. Instead decide ahead of time how much money you will be allowed on a weekly basis to spend on whatever you want, and try to stick to it.

First, consider what you need as opposed to what you want. Everything we spend falls into these two categories.

Our needs include the basics such as shelter, food, health, transportation, perhaps education, saving for the future and retirement, insurance and so on.

The area of wants is more fuzzy — chocolate doughnut, latte, new shoes, new car, new furniture, the latest gadgets, a boat, a motorcycle, appliances, that vacation in Florida or Las Vegas, smart phone, Netflix, cable TV, gym membership, and so on.

Wants are unique for each individual. My wants always included books. From the time when I was a child taking my allowance to the dime store to buy a comic book, I always wanted books. My book buying inclinations continued throughout my life. Buying the books for my courses in college and later seminary was always essential, but I constantly bought books whether in school or not, whatever my financial situation.

I usually read most of the books, but sometimes I bought more books than I could read or afford to pay for at the time, and even went into debt buying them with credit cards.

We all need to choose between what we want and what we need, and prioritize our spending. We have been living in an era where those lines have become blurred. Easy credit has given many of us an illusion that we deserve and can have everything we may want right now, but we do not have to pay the cost until later. It all looks so easy.

But eventually the credit card bills arrive. The card companies have lured us in with easy payment plans. Borrow $300, your payments are only $15 a month. Buy new furniture, and no payments for two years! Save on new carpet now!

My father in law used to say, "It's not a bargain if you don't need it."

You see it all boils down to that contest— what we need versus what we want. We each have an inner child inside of us that desires the latest toy. We crave what is new and bright and shiny. Our needs and wants compete for priority in our lives, and when we indulge our wants too often, there is not enough money left to pay for our needs, and suddenly we're living in chaos.

To escape your financial turmoil, you must bring the spending for your wants under control. You must be able to choose between your needs and your wants. The question is, after paying for what you need, how many of your wants can you afford?

When you see something you want you must determine if you can afford it now, and if not, then it will have to wait until you have funds available to pay for it.

Your spending plan can help you decide when you should buy something. Instead of buying something immediately, it will be necessary to postpone making the purchase until you are sure that you have enough on hand to pay for it without debting. Meanwhile, you can make a wish list for those things you might want to buy if you could afford them. Delayed gratification is a means of avoiding impulse buying. There's nothing wrong with desiring something. What causes problems is our giving in to the impulse to buy something right now that we really can't afford just because we want it. Being able to have the self discipline to delay gratification is an essential step in taking charge of our spending.

If you want to succeed with your financial recovery plan, then you simply must learn to delay gratification and make it a habit that you practice every day.

5 Pay Yourself First

*"Certainly there are lots of things in life that
money won't buy, but it's very funny—
Have you ever tried to buy them without money?"* —Ogden Nash

Your first priority must be to provide for your own basic needs-- food, shelter, transportation, and health. But some times when our finances get out of whack, we forget the basics. When bill collectors are constantly calling and demanding immediate payment, our priorities can get confused.

Once the bills have reached unmanageable proportions, it becomes impossible to satisfy all of our creditors' demands without neglecting our own necessities. We may then start to economize in ways that we should not. We skip changing the oil in our car, postpone going to the doctor or dentist, stop getting a prescription filled, and go without insurance on our health, home or car. We get wet feet when it rains because our shoes have holes in them. At the grocery store we buy mostly starchy foods or Spam, ramen noodles, boxed macaroni and cheese while skimping on fruits and vegetables.

But living on a diet of ramen noodles is not the solution, even if bill collectors are badgering you for payments, implying that you must be some kind of no-good, low account, worthless lowly worm.

It is essential to keep our perspective on what is most important. If you are to be successful in transforming your financial chaos into order, paying yourself first must be at the top of your list. Taking care of yourself and your family must be your number one priority. Good self care includes such items as eating balanced meals, health and dental care, adequate clothing, as well as maintenance of your home and car.

If your monthly expenses including your debts exceed your monthly resources, stop paying the debts for the time being and instead concentrate on meeting your basic needs first, including shelter, sustenance, health and transportation. Relax. Give yourself a break. Give yourself credit for what you are doing. We all make mistakes. The important thing is recognizing them, and making a new start and moving forward.

Be a Saver

Establish a habit of regular saving. If you want to get out of debt and stay out of debt, saving must become the essential foundation of your financial turnaround strategy. Make saving a regular habit. Save a portion of every pay check in a savings account. It can be either a set amount or a percentage of your income. I recommend that you aim to save 10% of all your income. Initially the money that you save here will be your emergency fund. This money will be a cushion for you, so that you can stop borrowing money. If you can save 10% of all your earnings, you will be taking a first step toward financial security. If you can't save 10% right away, start with a smaller amount, such as 5%, then gradually increase it over time until you reach the goal of 10% Saving must be the cornerstone of your new Financial Plan.

At first saving may be difficult, because you are already financially stretched, but once you get in the habit of not having that money to spend, you will find ways to stretch what you have to live on each month. Go back to your list of expenditures, and look at those items you have highlighted as non-essential. When you eliminate some or all of these things, you will find more money to use for paying down your debts and saving. You can either put the 10% into a savings account each time you are paid, or if you have your paycheck deposited electronically, your bank can set up an automatic payment into the savings account. You may want to consider opening a savings account in a different bank from where your checking account is. Having the savings where it takes a few days to transfer funds to your checking will discourage you from using it to cover impulse buying. The foundation of your basic financial freedom plan is savings. Your ability to save by cutting back on the total amount you've been spending each month will be the key to your success.

If you're ever going to get beyond living paycheck to paycheck, one essential requirement is establishing some savings. The first reason to save is to create your Emergency Fund.

The Emergency Fund is a contingency fund that you will use for paying unexpected, unplanned expenses with cash instead of relying on credit cards. It is not the pizza fund, the new shoes fund, night-out fund or the casino fund. It is the money you will set aside for an unexpected repair, new pair of glasses or one-time expense that is not included in your regular monthly Spending Plan.

Your first savings account will be your Emergency Fund. A good goal for the Emergency Fund will be to eventually build a balance of enough money to live on for 3 months. You can also start additional savings accounts for other purposes, such as a down payment for car, vacation, or Christmas club for buying gifts.

Be Frugal 34 Ways to Save Money —
Make a list for shopping, (and take it along with you to the store.)
Take a calculator along when you shop.
Shop at dollar stores
Buy it used in thrifts, garage sales, charity bazaars
Use coupons.
Walk.
Ride a bike
Eat in.
Learn to cook your own meals.
Use cloth napkins.
Take public transportation if you can.
Install a programmable thermostat.
Have an energy audit done on your home.
Use a clothesline or drying racks to air dry laundry.
Turn off the lights when you aren't in the room
Turn off computers if not in use.
Unplug all electronics, chargers, digital picture frames, etc. when not in use.
Use energy saving light bulbs.
When you don't have money, postpone going to the store.
Purchase used cars.
Use a water filter instead of buying bottled water.
Drink water instead of soda.
Plant a vegetable garden.
Don't use bundled cable-phone-internet provider subscriptions.
Have only basic telephone service.
Have only basic cable TV, or use an antenna if you're close enough to the transmitter.
Buy and use a pre-paid phone card for long distance.
Get a pre-paid cell phone plan.
Limit cell phone extras like text messaging and internet.
Borrow books and other media from the library.

Use homemade cleaning products — baking powder for scouring and stain removal, vinegar for general cleaning, window washing.
Recycle used gift wrap.
Volunteer for charities in lieu of donating money.
Give gifts of helpfulness to family and friends.

6 One Step at a Time

"Be bold, and mighty forces will come to your aid." — Basil King

Pay as you go.
To get off the monthly bill payment treadmill, you must stop using credit cards immediately if not sooner. Go cold turkey. Take all of your credit cards, cut them in half and put them in the garbage. That is the best way to dispose of them and remove the temptation to ever use one again.

Ok, you may find that idea difficult if not impossible. If you've been dependent on credit to make up any cash shortfalls, giving up your credit cards entirely may sound too drastic. At this point you may not be able to imagine getting by without them. The credit card philosophy is one of encouraging you to have a mind set of paying later. The policy of buy now, pay later is what got you into this mess.

Pay as you go is the way out. You must break the habit of using unsecured debt to pay for anything. You will have to learn a new habit, to never buy anything that you can not pay for with cash. Instead of using credit cards, you can use the debit card from your checking account when you shop. Debit cards do have some drawbacks. Shopping with a debit card can be tricky if you don't have a large minimum balance. Purchasing items with a debit card can lead to vagueness, as you will be trying to keep in mind the approximate amount of your available balance. Debit cards can also be less secure, as hackers can breach the store or gas station pump, get your card number and drain your account, or steal your identity. Use online banking to monitor your account frequently during the week, so that you're always aware of your balance. Notify the bank immediately if you hear of any stores where you used your card that have been hacked, or if you see any suspicious withdrawals.

Keeping a close watch over your checking account balance also helps you to avoid overdrafts and hefty overdraft charges.

Watch out for offers of "free" gift cards that require you to provide your card number. These are scams that may be enrolling you for bogus subscriptions that will be charged to your card.

An alternative strategy to using debit cards for local shopping trips is to plan in advance the amount of money you have to spend, and withdraw cash from your checking account to use for your purchases. Make a list of only those items that you need right away. If you know that you only have $25.00 cash in your wallet, you will be sure to only spend that much.

Keep a petty cash fund in your home to pay for any unexpected items that may be needed when your funds are low. You might save all of your change every week or add a dollar a week to the fund.

Another strategy is to withdraw the cash on paydays to cover shopping until the next payday. You can have envelopes for different categories, such as gas, groceries, clothing, household, pet, etc. Designate amounts from your Spending Plan to put into each envelope. You may not use each category every month, for example clothing, but perhaps you may add a bit to it.

Let's take a minute to review the steps we've just covered:

1. Keep track of all the money that you spend in a written record.
2. Save a percentage of all your income.
3. Create a Spending Plan to show all necessary expenses and savings each month
4. Find ways to economize by cutting back on spending for extras such as bottled water, soda, dining away from home, lottery tickets, DVD rentals, music downloads, extra services on cell phone plans, cable or satellite TV, internet access, other types of entertainment, sporting events, subscriptions, gym memberships and so on.
5. Redirect the money that you saved in Step 3 to paying down debts and bills.

You have now accomplished another important task — evaluating your monthly expenses as well as your available resources to meet them. You have created a Spending Plan to help you regain control of your finances.

You are already making progress. You have faced the facts about your financial situation, made a decision to take charge of your financial future, evaluated your assets and liabilities, reviewed your spending habits, listed your resources, and created a monthly Spending Plan.

Next we will continue that process as we add more details to the plan.

Now, go back to the decision you made, and review your Statement of Purpose. Your Statement of Purpose is very important, so you will want to review it every day.

7 Crunch Time

"The rich rule over the poor and the borrower is servant to the lender."-- Proverbs 22:7

The next step to becoming debt free is creating and implementing a Master Plan for paying off your debts. While you were reviewing your bills and debts, you made a list of the minimum payments due for each one on a monthly basis. The problem with making minimum payments on credit card debt is that almost the entire payment goes just for interest. If you only pay the required minimum monthly payment, your debt will not be reduced very quickly, even if you have stopped increasing it because you no longer use the card.

The credit card companies make their profits by collecting interest on the money you owe. They lure people in with offers of zero interest, low balance transfers and small minimum payments. Many consumers fail to read all of the fine print in the contract, where the hidden charges and penalties lurk, that can be added in later that can keep them trapped on a debt treadmill forever.

When it comes to credit card or any other unsecured debt, such as department stores like Wal-Mart, J.C. Penny's, Best Buy or Target; gasoline companies, like Mobil, Shell or BP, home improvement cards, or Home Depot, the deck is stacked against those consumer who do not pay off their balances in full each month.

Whenever you can't pay for something in cash right away, and you have used revolving credit instead, you'll end up paying far more in the long run for the item that you bought on sale and paid for with a plastic card. In fact, you'll pay far more because you will be charged compound interest on the balance for the remainder of time you carry the debt.

By carrying a loan balance over time, the amount you will pay in interest increases the total cost of the item you purchased. The total amount you will pay depends on the amount you borrow, together with the interest on the balance due that is charged to you on a daily basis. The combination of relatively high interest rates plus low minimum payments creates a profit bonanza for the lender, and a losing scenario for the borrower.

You lose because in the long run you end up paying more for anything that you bought on credit than you would have paid for the same item with cash. And also, the payments you are required to make to pay down your card balances constantly drain your current financial resources, so that you lack funds to pay for things you need today and tomorrow.

The following table provides a snapshot of how much a borrower pays for several accounts. The accounts are calculated at a 3% amount for a minimum balance, which may be higher or lower than minimum balances on accounts you owe, and typical interest percentage rates, which may be either higher or lower than yours.

The table shows the total amount you would pay, assuming you pay only the minimum balance each month, without adding any additional charges to the balance due, along with the length of time in months it would take to pay each balance.

Of course, if you continue to use the card and make additional charges to the balance each month, then the eventual payoff amount grows ever higher, and the time to repay the balance expands accordingly, keeping you on a never-ending treadmill.

Sample Bills & Payoff Time at Minimum Payment

Account	Balance	% Interest	Payment	Pay-off	Total
Visa	$570	19.99	$17.10	50 mo.	$839
Master	$710	18.99	$21.30	48 mo	$1017
Am Exp	$980	21.99	$29.40	52 mo	$1528
Disc	$2960	21.99	$88.80	52 mo.	$4615
Gas	$280	19.99	$8.40	20 mo.	$331
Store	$560	19.99	$16.80	50 mo	$824

This table is an example to show how much more you will pay altogether by only paying only the minimum monthly payment, as well as how long it takes to pay off bills this way.

Make your own list or chart that shows each credit or store card and the balance due. You may want to also note the interest rate currently being charged as well as the day of the month the payment is due. It is important to make your payment on time to avoid being charged late fees and higher interest.

You can use the table as a guide for setting up a Master Plan for Debt Disposal.

By following a plan you will begin by paying the minimum payment on all of your bills except Gasoline Card each month. Since Gasoline Card has the lowest balance, you would begin to pay that off first. Pay as much as you possibly can manage toward the Gasoline Card bill, using the extra money that you have found by reducing your spending. If the minimum payment on Gasoline Card is $8.40, then pay $25 a month if you can, using money that you save by eliminating unnecessary spending.

Continue doing this every month, always paying the maximum amount you can possibly manage to pay, until the balance is totally paid in full.

Once the Gasoline Card is paid off, you tackle the Department Store card which has the next lowest balance due on your chart, by rolling the Gasoline Card payment onto its minimum, thus speeding up your payoff time for its balance. Continue the process until all of your debt is eliminated.

Always pay your smallest bill first. Gradually by doing this, you will reduce the total number of payments you must make each month. If you have any small miscellaneous bills lingering, pay them as quickly as possible.

Then once you have eliminated the debt, you can redirect the money you were paying toward the debts to saving and investing for your future.

8 Complications and Trade Offs

"When you come to the end of your rope, tie a knot and hang on." — Franklin D. Roosevelt

What can you do if your financial evaluation reveals that you have any no extra money left after meeting your expenses, or even worse, that your monthly obligations are greater than your resources, including all of your income? You have reviewed your spending and cut out extras, but a huge gap remains between what you have and what you owe. The shortfall may result from any one or combination of reasons. Perhaps you or your spouse had to take a cut in pay due to a loss of job or reduction of hours. Or you may have large medical bills that weren't covered by insurance. You may have consistently been spending more than you earn, resulting in high debts on unsecured loans, such as credit cards.

If this is your situation, one possibility is to negotiate better repayment terms with your creditors. Start by contacting the companies or providers that you owe. Explain your circumstances and tell them that you will need more time to pay your bills, and in the meantime you want to work out a more affordable payment plan until you can get back on your feet.

Let them know that you are attempting to resolve all of your debts as soon as possible. They should be willing to work with you if they understand that you sincerely want to resolve the debts.

If you are receiving harassing phone calls from bill collectors, and talking with them on the telephone seems too intimidating, write a letter instead. Try writing one letter each week until all of your creditors have been contacted. Writing letters as a way of communication can be less threatening, plus some companies will be more responsive to written communication.

As you begin taking action this way, you will begin to feel more control over your situation, even if you aren't able to make payments. You have taken initiative to reach a resolution, and now the creditors should be cooperative. When creditors call, take a deep breath and tell them that you are in a rough spot now but are trying to get your finances in order and will have to get back to them later. Then hang up. It is best to avoid conversations with collectors who are trying to get information about your financial situation and pressure you. You do not have to give any information to anyone on the phone, nor do you have to put up with harassment and abuse.

Try to keep the lines of communication open with your creditors. When they see that you are acting in good faith, they will be more reasonable as well. After all, since they have to pay collection agencies, collections are costly for the business. Always try to think win – win.

You may be able to raise some cash by selling assets such as vehicles or a boat. If you are making large car payments, you might be able to sell the car and buy a less expensive used car to replace it. Some times it's not possible to do this if there is not a market for the vehicle. Like real estate, vehicles can be difficult to liquidate.

In this situation, you may try to negotiate with your lender for lower payments, or even consider surrendering the vehicle by letting them repossess it. In the short term, of course, this is bad for your credit rating, but your credit rating may not be that good any way, and you may have no choice.

Perhaps you could sell other assets such as motorcycles, jewelry, coin collections, sports memorabilia, exercise equipment, electronic gadgets or furniture.

Depending on how much stuff you have, this can potentially be a good source for cash. Some people have raised thousands of dollars selling their extras on eBay, Craig's List or garage sales.

If you own your home and you have greater equity than what you owe, it may be possible to sell the home and rent instead, depending on the area of the country where you live, and what the real estate market is there at the present time.

9 Get Help If You Need It

"Insanity: doing the same thing over and over again and expecting different results." - Albert Einstein

By now you should have a realistic picture of your financial situation, and will have worked out your Spending Plan. You have made a decision to get your finances in order, save money, and pay down your debt.

Yet those steps may not satisfy your creditors. As a consumer, you are legally protected from unreasonable harassment by bill collectors. The Fair Debt Collection Practices Act (FDCPA) is a federal law which prohibits debt collectors from using abusive, unfair, or deceptive practices to collect from you. The Federal Trade Commission (FTC), the US consumer protection agency, enforces FDCPA.

The Act covers personal, family, and household debts, including money that you owe on personal credit card accounts, auto loans, medical bills, and your mortgage. The FDCPA does not cover any debts you incurred to run a business.

The law prohibits debt collectors' calls at inconvenient times, between 9 pm and 8 am, calls to you at work, abusive or threatening language, and other tactics.

If a collector has continued to call you after you have spoken to them and explained that you are trying to resolve the debt or intend to work out a settlement, you can write them a letter requesting they stop calling. Keep a copy of your letter, and send it by certified mail so that you have a record of delivery.

A Kentucky consumer was awarded a settlement in excess of $2,500 after he had been subjected to repeated calls and harassment at work and home by Creditors Interchange, a collection agency for Bank of America credit card.

Creditors Interchange sought to embarrass the man by using tactics such as:
  An untrue statement that the collector was a Bank of America employee
  Falsely claiming that the collector had placed a 'fraud alert' in the consumer's 'record'
  False threats of arbitration/litigation
  False threats of wage garnishment and bank levies.

The debtor was a client of a consumer action network, which advised him of his rights and advised the man to record all debt collector contacts in a call log. After he had gathered written statements and evidence from potential witnesses he was referred to an attorney who was knowledgeable regarding the FDCPA for his legal claim.
The settlement was quickly granted, and in addition the collection agency was required to pay all of the legal fees incurred in the matter.
In Texas a debtor obtained a settlement after filing an action for collection harassment with the help of a FDCPA attorney in the same network.
The debtor, who was enrolled in a debt settlement program, began to receive harassing phone calls from a debt collection agency representing a major credit card company.
The collector harassed the woman at her place of employment, and even placed calls to her superiors and HR department in an attempt to embarrass and humiliate her.
The debtor had documented evidence in the form of voice mail messages that the collection agency had left for her which included statements such as:
"We are retained to file proceedings against the two of you in County Court."
"We are contacting you voluntarily regarding two very serious allegations that have been issued…serious enough that we were compelled by Texas state laws to contact the Attorney General's office."
"I'm scheduled to file the legal proceedings with the court clerk either tomorrow or Friday."

If you are not comfortable with negotiating with creditors yourself, you might consider these options:

Seek out a credit counselor who will work with you and may be able to negotiate better terms than you can. The credit counselor can help you set up a monthly payment arrangement with your creditors. Most credit counselors will charge you a percentage of your payments for their services.

Debt Settlement Companies negotiate settlements of unsecured debt, such as credit cards, on your behalf. They charge fees for their services, which include placing your funds in an escrow account, which will then be used to pay off the creditors.

You should approach such firms with extreme caution as some are fraudulent enterprises that have taken money from unwary consumers, without ever negotiating any settlements on their behalf, and then even disappearing with their funds.

There are some legitimate debt settlement companies. It is important to carefully investigate any company fully before you undertake any such contract. Some important considerations are how long the company has been in business, what accreditations or affiliations it has; and most importantly how much it charges for the service.

Ask them to provide a detailed account of any fees you are required to pay, and when they will be paid. Some companies charge upfront and deduct their fees at the beginning of the contract period, prior to building up the balance in your escrow account.

Ask for business references such as the Better Business Bureau. You may inquire with your state Attorney General Office of Consumer Protection to see if the firm is licensed in your state, and if there are any complaints about their business practices.

The Association of Settlement Companies, TASC, is the largest trade association serving the debt settlement industry. TASC members voluntarily agree to comply with TASC's strict industry standards. Any company you choose should be a member.

It is also possible to reach settlements on your own of course, though such negotiations may not be for the fainthearted. When filmmaker and author Ken Golde owed over $200,000 in credit card debt, he was able to successfully negotiate his own settlements with the card companies down from $212,000 to $30,000.

Golde said, "I was paying nearly $4000 a month in interest. I was afraid. I was ashamed. I withdrew from my family and friends. I couldn't see a way out of this debt. "All I found were companies who advertised they could do it for me for a fee and it seemed they wanted me to believe I couldn't do it myself so that I would pay them. Every person out there is the C.E.O. of their own corporation, the corporation of 'You.' And you have the right to deal with finance and debt without emotion or judgment, the same way other businesses do."

Golde published a book about his experience, The Do-It-Yourself Bailout: How I Reduced My Credit Card Debt from $212,000 to $30,000 in Six Months.

Debtors Anonymous is a twelve-step program founded on the principles of Alcoholics Anonymous. DA offers a supportive community of other debtors who are achieving solvency by attending meetings and practicing the DA recovery principles. For more information on DA, see the Resource section at the end of this book.

10 Is Bankruptcy an Option?

"Pay every debt as if God wrote the bill." — Emerson
If you find yourself buried under a crushing load of debt that seems overwhelming, you may be tempted to file for bankruptcy. When the economy tanked in 2007-08, following the mortgage meltdown, housing crash, and then the recession, the number of individuals who filed for personal bankruptcy rose sharply.
According to a report by the Reuters news agency, bankruptcy filings in the US rose by 31 percent in 2008 for both businesses and individuals.
Total bankruptcy filings rose to 1,117,771, the Administrative Office of U.S. Courts said, up from 850,912 in 2007.
The total is nearly twice the 617,660 filings recorded in 2006, when an overhaul in bankruptcy laws led to a drop in filings.
Businesses accounted for 43,546 filings in 2008, a small percentage of the total, but up 54 percent from 2007.
The number of filings rose steadily throughout 2008 as the economy worsened, according to figures released by the agency, which oversees federal courts.
Filings rose under Chapters 7, 11, and 13 of the bankruptcy code, but filings under Chapter 12, a category for farmers, fell 8 percent.
It is best to seek legal advice and counsel to better understand your options, including bankruptcy. Generally bankruptcy attorneys offer a consultation for free. However individuals filing for bankruptcy are required to pay the attorney's fees in advance as well as the required court filing fees.

While bankruptcy may offer the debtor some relief, its primary purpose was intended for extreme circumstances such as catastrophic losses or extremely large medical bills. A study of personal bankruptcies that was published in 2005 by Harvard University researchers cited illness and medical bills as the leading cause of half of the 1,458,000 personal bankruptcies in 2001. The report, which was published by the journal Health Affairs, estimated that medical bankruptcies were affecting about 2 million Americans annually, counting debtors and their dependents, including about 700,000 children.

Surprisingly, most of those bankrupted by illness had health insurance. More than three-quarters were insured at the start of the bankrupting illness. However, 38 percent had lost coverage at least temporarily by the time they filed for bankruptcy.

Most of the medical bankruptcy filers were middle class; 56 percent owned a home and the same number had attended college. In many cases, illness forced breadwinners to take time off from work -- losing income and job-based health insurance precisely when families needed it most.

Families in bankruptcy suffered many privations -- 30 percent had a utility cut off and 61 percent went without needed medical care.

In the long term bankruptcy is a lose - lose solution and should be considered only as a last resort if there is no other way out. While filing for bankruptcy may seem to be a solution, it has many long-lasting consequences that affect your future financial options, such as eligibility for loans, mortgages or other credit.

Bankruptcy will not free you from student loan or tax obligations.

11 THE COURAGE TO CHANGE

"There can be no freedom or beauty about a home life that depends on borrowing and debt." -- Henrik Ibsen

Debt and the financial chaos that result from it are caused by a variety of problems, from simple disorganization, carelessness, to unemployment, working at low wage jobs, to addictions such as Shopaholism, or Compulsive Shopping Disorder, drugs and alcohol or gambling.

Shopaholism has reached epidemic proportions in the US. About 5.8% of the US population, or over 15 million Americans were estimated to be compulsive buyers, according to a study published in the Journal of Psychiatry in October, 2006. More recently, research results from the Journal of Consumer Research (Dec. 2008) stated that there may be as many as 8.9% or over 25 million shopping addicts in the US.

If you think you have been a compulsive buyer or shopper, you may need to find help and support to overcome your spending urges, if you do not want to find yourself falling back into the same habits in the future.

Some of us learned unhelpful attitudes about money and debt while we were growing up.

Our parents may have struggled with their own financial issues, and didn't model good financial habits or teach us about saving and financial responsibility. Perhaps they were always working and never had conversations about money with us. Consequently we were not well prepared to understand the basics of financial management. We lacked the ability and experience to understand the risk involved with credit, and all the potential negative consequences that could result from getting entangled with it.

Whatever the origin of your financial distress, overcoming your problems will take time. It takes time to unlearn habits that we want to replace, and to learn any new behavior or skills. We must practice consistently until it becomes a regular part of our daily routine.

Daily mindfulness is essential whenever we want to change anything, whether it is losing a few pounds, getting more exercise, or mastering our finances.

At first we may feel overwhelmed with details. Sometimes we may get discouraged by the size of the task. We may forget to keep up with our record keeping, and get off track. It's normal whenever we try to unlearn bad habits and replace them with positive ones. If that happens, just resume your routine. Gradually it will get easier and easier, and you will see more progress.

The good news is, change is possible. We can learn from our mistakes, and liberate ourselves from the past. We have the power to start over, make more prudent choices and learn the skills we need to master our money. By taking control over our finances on a daily basis, we can get free and clear and escape the debt trap for good.

12 THE UNBROKEN CIRCLE

*"Earn as much as you can,
Save as much as you can,
Give as much as you can."*– John Wesley

Money is only a tool, a means of exchange. In and of itself money is neither good nor bad. Scripture says, "For the love of money is a root of all kinds of evil." – 1 Tim. 6:10 This verse is often misquoted as, money is the root of all evil, however that was not the intent of its author, who added in the next verse, "Some people, eager for money, have wandered from the faith and pierced themselves with many griefs." It was not the money that caused them grief, but their obsession with it. To recognize that money is only one part of life puts money in its rightful place because your economic health involves much more than mere finances. Beyond the material objects in our lives that money represents, there is a spiritual dimension. Because of the power and potential it has to control us, money is a spiritual issue.

As we have become aware that money is a spiritual matter, we begin to recognize our connections with our neighbors, whether they are in our local community or in distant country. In fact it is an essential element of our own well-being to find ways to be connected to others by giving to help those in need.

Being frugal and careful with money does not mean we should be cheap. No matter what our financial situation may be, it is always possible to give something to some worthwhile cause that is greater than yourself. Buy a few extra grocery items for the food pantry. You can de-clutter your home and donate unused household items to thrift shops. Throw some spare change into a charity's collection jar.

"Give, and it will be given to you. A good measure, pressed down, shaken together and running over, will be poured into your lap. For with the measure you use, it will be measured to you."– Luke. 6:38

Many people have found the tithe to be a useful standard for their charitable giving. I was deeply in debt when I first heard a speaker at a finance workshop advocate tithing. I did not see how I could possibly tithe, when I had to make student loan payments. When I asked the speaker to clarify what he had said, his answer was, "When you tithe, the money stretches to the end of the month." I decided to try it as an experiment, thinking it could not be true, but it was. The first month passed, and then the second and the third. I was able to tithe and stay current on all of my bills.

In Scripture, the tithe was an offering of 10 per cent to be returned to God, as part of the law given to Moses:

"A tithe of everything from the land, whether grain from the soil or fruit from the trees, belongs to the Lord; it is holy to the Lord." (Lev. 27:30)

Interestingly, the law also required that the tithe, which was given to the Temple, was to be taken from the first fruits of the harvest.

The actual amount you decide to give is up to you of course, but the important idea is that you would designate a certain percentage of your income to be given on a regular basis to some worthwhile charitable mission that is important to you. If you are short on cash, perhaps you may want to donate time by volunteering instead. It is important to be connected to a cause that is greater than our self.

13 GRATITUDE – THANKSGIVING

> "He who receives a benefit with gratitude repays the first installment on his debt." —Seneca

Gratitude is an awareness of being grateful, knowing that I am blessed in countless ways. Gratitude gives me understanding, and makes me mindful of all that I have for which I am thankful, first of all for the many gifts of life, health, and strength which cannot be measured in purely material ways. I give thanks for all that has been given to me, for what I have received up to this point in time, but also what I will receive in the future. Not only have I already been blessed, but I am being blessed now, and will continue to be blessed as long as I live.

Gratitude says thank you, not only for what I have received that I wanted, but also for all I once thought I wanted that I did not receive.

A spirit of gratitude gives one feelings of contentment. When I am thankful for food, I can be satisfied with eating lentil beans and rice. I am able to appreciate hearing a bird song when I awaken, thankful for a new day. The apostle Paul expressed it this way:

"I have learned to be content whatever the circumstances. I know what it is to be in need, and I know what it is to have plenty. I have learned the secret of being content in any and every situation, whether well fed or hungry, whether living in plenty or want." —Philippians 4:11-12

As our chronic debt declines and our prosperity increases, we begin to realize our gratitude for everything. Our peace of mind is yet another reminder of changes we have made. Once we are no longer burdened by constant feelings of failure, scarcity, worry and inadequacy, we have serenity.

We are now increasingly able to devote our attention more completely to our work and family life. When our financial house is in order, we are no longer distracted by nagging financial concerns. As a result we are more conscientious with all of our responsibilities and we become more productive. We feel more capable and confident in all that we do.

As our efforts meet with success, our earnings increase. Because we have established routines for paying our debts and saving, our resources continue to increase. We build our reserves, but at the same time we would not want to forget where we came from and how we arrived at our more prosperous circumstances.

Take some time to reflect from your own spiritual perspective on the help you have received. In my tradition as a Christian, I would call that God's grace. "It is through grace you have been saved," Paul said.

Perhaps in your understanding you would call upon your Higher Power, God as you understand God. Consider the circumstances you were in, and the events that have happened in your life that have brought you to this point.

In my life's journey, God's grace has often come to me through other people—family, friends, pastor, colleagues, neighbors, mentors, counselors. Think of those persons who have met you along the way who reached out to help you when you were in need, who came and walked beside you on this journey. Perhaps you might like to thank them, and if so that is fine.

But thanking those who helped you may not be as important as finding ways of giving to others. The best way to give thanks is to give a gift to a cause beyond ourselves. Just as we have received and benefited from grace, so we are called to become channels of grace and help to others.

> Night is drawing nigh—
> For all that has been—Thanks!
> For all that shall be—Yes!
> --Dag Hammarskjold, (1905-61)

RESOURCES

Organizations
Debtors Anonymous is a twelve-step group that helps individuals to recover from problems with debt. There are chapters in many major metropolitan areas of the US and some foreign countries.

"Debtors Anonymous is a fellowship of men and women who share their experience, strength and hope with each other that they may solve their common problem and help others to recover from compulsive debting."

The only requirement for membership is a desire to stop incurring unsecured debt. There are no dues or fees for D.A. membership; we are self-supporting through our own contributions.

D.A. is not allied with any sect, denomination, politics, organization or institution; does not wish to engage in any controversy; neither endorses nor opposes any causes.

Our primary purpose is to stop debting one day at a time and to help other compulsive debtors to stop incurring unsecured debt." - Preamble of Debtors Anonymous, Revised and approved August 2003

Contact Information:
Debtors Anonymous General Service Office,
PO Box 920888, Needham, MA 02492-0009
Telephone toll Free: 800-421-2383 - US Only; 781-453-2743
Website: debtorsanonymous.org; email office@debtorsanyonymous.org

Gamblers Anonymous is a fellowship of men and women who share their experience, strength and hope with each other that they may solve their common problem and help others to recover from a gambling problem.

The only requirement for membership is a desire to stop gambling. There are no dues or fees for Gamblers Anonymous membership; we are self-supporting through our own contributions. Gamblers Anonymous is not allied with any sect, denomination, politics, organization or institution; does not wish to engage in any controversy; neither endorses nor opposes any cause. Our primary purpose is to stop gambling and to help other compulsive gamblers do the same.
Contact information:
Gamblers Anonymous International Service Office, PO Box 17173 Los Angeles CA 90017
(213) 386-8789, National Hotline: (888) 424-3577
Email: isomain@gamblersanonymous.org
Website: gamblersanonymous.org

The Association of Independent Credit Counseling Agencies is a national membership organization promoting quality and consistent delivery of credit counseling services. (866) 703-8787 toll free line for finding local non-profit credit counseling.
Website: www.aiccca.org/
National Foundation for Credit Counseling (800) 388-2227
Resources and information on debt, avoiding foreclosure, credit counseling and finding a credit counselor.
Website: www.nfcc.org
The National Endowment for Financial Education, NEFE is a non-profit foundation provides practical articles, worksheets, tips and valuable resources to help you understand and manage your money. 5299 DTC Blvd. Suite 1300 Greenwood Village, CO 80111, (303) 741-6333 or (303) 741-NEFE.
Website: www.smartaboutmoney.org
Online Resources
Budget Pulse, free budgeting software: www.budgetpulse.com
dsBudget Free software, versions for windows, mac, iOS, android

http://download.cnet.com/dsBudget/3000-2057_4-10766253.html

spendster.org is a website of NEFE (see above) where members can blog and upload videos about their overspending.

choosetosave.org is a personal finance information website sponsored by the Employee Benefit Research Institute that includes about 100 online calculators and money saving tips.

livingonadime.com: Free blog and frugal living tips on basic household expenses, information booklets for purchase.

The Illinois Institute for Addiction Recovery provides a quiz regarding shopaholism on its website, addictionrecov.org. Identification of four or more behaviors indicates a possible problem with shopping or spending.

shopaholicnomore.com: Website for shopping addicts by Dr. April Benson, a New York psychologist. Shopping questionnaire, books, articles and resources on compulsive over shopping.

shopaholicsanonymous.org is a division of the Shulman Center for Compulsive Theft and Spending, Terrence D. Shulman (248) 358-8508

Books

A Currency of Hope, Debtors Anonymous
Born to Lose: Memoirs of a Compulsive Gambler, Bill Lee
Debt Free Living, Larry Burkett
Bought Out and $pent! Recovery from Compulsive $hopping and $pending, Terrence D. Shulman
Giving and Tithing, Larry Burkett
I Shop, Therefore I Am: Compulsive Buying and the Search for Self, Dr. April Benson
It's Not About the Money: Unlock Your Money Type to Achieve Spiritual and Financial Abundance, Brent Kessel
Nicotine Dreams: A Story of Compulsive Gambling, Katie Cunningham
Thanks! How the New Science of Gratitude Can Make You Happier, Robert Emmons
The Do-It-Yourself Bailout: How I Reduced My Credit Card Debt from $212,000 to $30,000 in Six Months, Ken Golde
Think and Grow Rich, Napoleon Hill
To Buy or Not to Buy: Why We Overspend and How to Stop, Dr. April Benson
Turning the Tables on Gambling: Help and Hope for an Addictive Behavior, Dr. Gregory L. Jantz

ABOUT DEBORAH GORMAN

Deborah is a life coach and writer. She has been a journalist, pastor, teacher and entrepreneur. Her work has appeared in numerous publications.

Deborah is originally from the Midwestern US, and now makes her home in North Carolina. She enjoys hiking, gardening, travel and exploring new places.

She has published three ebooks:

Free and Clear How to Master Your Money and Escape the Debt Trap
The Essentials of Starting Your Business
How to Start a Business and Be Your Own CEO